The Myth of Age
And Time

D W Storer

The Myth of Age and Time

D W Storer

Illustrations by Sarah Storer

For Janet

Thank you for
being my friend
& all the help

Chapters

Introduction

This work isn't about getting old, or wondering where my childhood went, it's about discovering exactly where the years went, and why they passed without even the merest hint of a warning that they would do so secretively. '*Time*' is clearly not something to be trusted- it's unreliable, a cheat, and no matter what anyone says it will never be on your side. Age sneaks up, mocks us, and stabs us in the back- and that's something we should keep our eyes open for. You never know, there might well be some way to dodge the blow.

Once I tried
To go back home
But it stood there empty
Forgotten, alone
All that was left there
That I could see
Was the Wreckage of what
I once called 'me'

D W Storer

Dedication

To my wife Sarah- not just for her help and support but for the illustrations she provides for each of my books

My children, Sam, Adam, Peter, and Maddie

To my parents Bill and Shirley, and my sister Yvette

To my friends – for their help and support; Charlie Fairey of the Mystic Masque , Trish & Angie Portmann , Penny Midson, Leighann Parker, Annette Thompson, Catherine Rose, Katrina Isabel Johns, Janet D. B. Heaton-Ferguson, J Keith Landreth. Roni S. Healan, Sue Walkusky, Tim Fowler, Karen Abear, Sheila Shailes, Kat Morrow-Hughes, Tie Soliwoda, Troy Breimon, Inga Butcher, Lesley Ann Jackson, Zara Blackstone, Maria Lefcovitch, Terry Anne Barbour, Marie Elliot, Catherine Nordstrom, George Ceridwen, and all of our friends on Faecesbook.

If by some chance you, whoever you are reading this, know me from the past why not give me a call? You can find me on Facebook·easily enough and it would be great to hear from you.

D W Storer

Where are my yesteryears?

I sat, in my kitchen, watching the rain and wondered at how it was that so many people I know are so afraid of age, or getting older, whereas my own fear is somewhat different. What if all my memories are only imagine, if none of those people I knew, the places I went to, the voices I heard and faces I saw only ever existed in my mind? A curious notion, perhaps, but nevertheless it calls into question the nature of reality as we perceive it and, since the faculty of perception itself is not the most reliable, then what is real or merely a figment of my imagination?

I die each day
Yet come the morrow
Still I'll roam
On time I've borrowed
My shadow's missing
Still reminiscing
Who dares to walk
With me?

Time- what is it? A theory, a loose term, used to describe the atrophy of physical existence- But what if there is more to it than just the physical? Where do these memories come from? Contrariwise, could it be possible that I am still a child and this is all a dream? Consider – I may be seeing my life in advance and have no way to change it- or have I already?

It's a short bus ride to suicide
Where the bright young things never walk but glide
And no-ones happy
Or even sad
It's a walk down the street of Forgotten Names
Where nothing has changed
But it's not the same
Yet the games we once played there
Still make us glad
It never rains there
The sun doesn't shine
Is this just all in my head?
Who's voices are these that tell me who I should be?

In tired worn out shoes
Sat reading the news
Taking the views
We memories choose

Maybe it's a sign of getting old
Because nowadays I really notice the cold
But I can see myself
And still laugh
Now my brother's back home
Living with our mother
All the drink and drugs left him in the gutter
Crying,' life is rough'
Well, that's just tough
It never rains here
The sun doesn't shine
Is this just all in my head?
Where forgotten voices still tell me who I should be

In tired worn out shoes
Sat reading the news
Taking the views
We memories lose

When and Why?

It was on a trip to visit my father - back in Mitcham, the town of my birth, that it hit me. Not the thought of age, and how things change, but of what happened to those years that caused them to vanish so? I didn't notice their passing, and in truth 'time' isn't something I've ever worried about anyway, but I did ask myself where had all the sights, and sounds, or even the people, I knew go?

Walking about the town, trying to follow familiar paths, in an attempt to recall the thoughts and experiences that I'd once had there, and maybe even come across an old friend or two, it soon became clear that it just wasn't going to happen. It was merely a place I'd once known yet now only existed in my memories- the changes were too great, everything I came across only left me feeling like a stranger. My home was no longer my home- perhaps it never had been.

There then lies the question, and it led to the seeds of this book, when did the change occur and why? When we look, as children, to the future it may well be that not only do we not recognize it when it is taking place but find it to be more so that we, ourselves, have become the past.

Walking along the old Church Road
Rain falling down
Bitterly cold
The whole place had changed
Nothing was the same
They'd destroyed everything
I'd hoped to see my old home
The place where as a kid
I had grown
Before I'd gone away
But there was nothing I could say
They'd destroyed everything
Once upon a time there I was so happy
Playing in the park and the old abbey
But I should have known
There's no going home
Back then when the future was calling
I couldn't say if I was climbing or falling
But with the urge to roam
There's no going home
It's not the place that I remember
No spring or summer there,
Only the winter
Not even those hazy autumn days
That seem so far away
Now they've destroyed everything
In tired old shoes on worn out feet
I walked those roads
And down the streets
Looking for familiar faces
Or maybe even traces
But I couldn't find anything
Once upon a time there I was so happy
Playing in the park and the old abbey
But I should have known
There's no going home
Back then when the future was calling
I couldn't say if I was climbing or falling
But once you start to roam
There's no going home

***

Think of soul
That prone to roam
Knows of neither
Hearth nor home
Unremembered
Oft dismembered
Unheard, unknown
And quite alone

***

I cannot show you where I lived
For it exists no more
And the shadows of we who grew up there
Have moved to some far distant shore

***

Deflections and Deceptions

To be mortal
Is well and fine
But to be a God
Would be Divine

It's hard to say if I have what you may call a 'religion'. In truth I don't pray to , or even revere , any particular deity - choosing instead to talk to whichever spirits are present in whatever place I happen to find myself . Is it strange to do so? Reactions to my admitting this range from the merely incredulous to expressions of outrage, and those accompanying accusations, or nods of approval, can vary just as wildly also. Am I an oddity, a heretic, a fool, or just a dreamer? Or am I something else?

I speak with those
Who speak to me
And observe all
They let me see

If I were to be pressed on the matter then , yes , I'd admit to believing in the existence of Gods - in fact I've never denied them , although questioning their methods and reasons is probably what led me here in the first place . Where is here? A good question, albeit one that can't be answered with any accuracy and that's the truth. I am not, in any way, comfortable with the 'modern world ' - to say I feel lost at the best of times would be an understatement. I have no understanding of this age, and I don't intend to try - it's probably better that way.

I often find I'm walking
Through the streets that form my mind
Sometimes there it's raining
Sometimes the weather's fine
There's no reason to be walking
For I could surely find a ride
But in truth it's just a pleasant way
To while away the time

I met a stranger there
He was holding up a sign -
That read, 'How can you ever get there,
'If you can't walk in a straight line?'
I paid him no attention
Because I wander where I will
For in truth it's just a pleasant way
To while away the time

My walking stick tapped out
A tune on the cobble stones
Reminding me perhaps
I should make my way back home
So I lit my cigarette
And in blue grey cloud so fine
Tried to think of better ways
To while away my time

***

I don't believe in heaven
Or even any hell
But I do believe in 'now'
Perhaps it's just as well

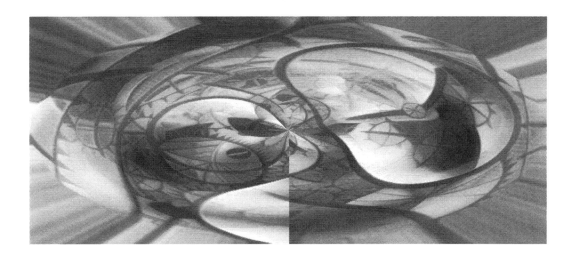

Watching the Clock

What is it I need to remember, and what things do I need to forget? Why is it that I don't notice my age yet, perversely, feel 'old'? What if '*today*' is all that exists and there really is no past or future? Ageless in age, we persist in the hope that today will be eternal for when it ends what can we find except that tomorrow is a myth?

I was born under yesteryear's sky
I tell the truth though sometimes I lie
I knew a child who watched with eyes open wide
He walked through the years, got old - then he died
All those years passed are getting harder to find
Each one has left its scar

So many tell me what they're going to do
I don't hold my breath, it's nothing new
Promises that seem to sprout up like weeds
Just float away like dandelion seeds
As my hopes and dreams fade I know that I'll find
Each one has left its scar

In worn out shoes I sit and take in the views
It's ok but not the life I would choose
There are far better ways to spend my day
But unless you're there then you've got nothing to say
I've got my reasons but I can't decide
Why each one must leave a scar?

I shall follow my path
Right to its end
And I know there I'll find
That it will extend
Far, far, beyond
All I'd thought to see
Yet never had dreamed
What it could be
So I shall walk on
Alone and forlorn
Still not understanding
Why I had been born

***

When, at last,
I looked out of my window
Yesterday's pains
Rose in a crescendo

***

My memories
Are beyond compare
Though into them
I rarely dare
For childhood I
Had barely discovered
Before I learned
It could not be recovered

Time on My Hands

I have a watch, several in fact, and I like to look at them- especially those that I can see the inside of. I keep them wound up, polished, and safe from careless hands yet I don't actually use them. Time itself, in my life at least, seems not to rely on the passing of seconds or minutes but of years.

I had no reason to be waiting
For the coming day
But I did so hoping answers
Might just come my way
And if by chance they did
Would they on my conscience play?
For I had so many questions
That I knew not how to say
Come the day
Would I understand the 'why'?
Come the day
Would I fall or would I fly?
Come the day

My life it would be fleeting
As was my right to stay
But I knew that if I left
I would never learn to play
A mist did then come rolling in
Obscuring the sun
And as the words there echoed briefly
I knew I'd soon be gone
Come the day
Would I understand the 'why'?
Come the day
Why does the fire flare then die?
Come the day

I found that I was nowhere
In a place that could not be
Quietly staring out into
A vast and silent sea
Moonlight and the stars
Revealed a dying tree
That yearned to cast a shadow
As it stood there forlornly
Come the night
What was left for me to say?
Come the night
Not even echoes now did play
Come the night

I stood a while beside myself
There was much I wished to say
But before I said a word
I watched myself walking away
The rolling waves departed then
Not even they would stay
All that remained were idols
And they were made of clay
Come the night
With no reason left to stay
Come the night
Even shadows stayed away
Come the night

My soul is but a candle flame
That dances and does play
Upon unseen winds that quietly
Send me on my way
My thoughts are wild and varied
They change each word I'd say
And if Fate decides to fortune me
I'll be leaving here today
Come the day
Would I understand the 'why'?
Come the day
Would I fall or would I fly?
Come the day

I am but a leaf
That has fallen from the tree
Hoping before I go to ground
I will reach epiphany
This world to me makes no sense
Was I ever meant to be?
For between those mixed up colours
There are so many shades of grey
Come the night
I'll be leaving here today
Come the night
I'll be far away
Come the day

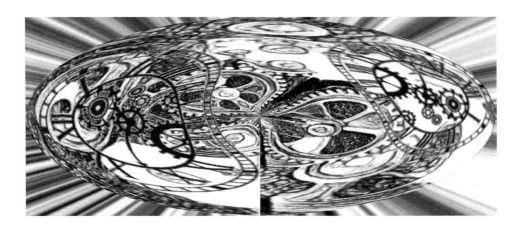

Thoughts of the Night

Being a true insomniac getting to sleep is no problem, but staying that way… now that's a different story altogether, and all sorts of notions float about on the sea of semi-consciousness that I drift in and out of in the attempt to work out what the hell is going on. Of course, if I do find an answer I forget it as soon as I fall asleep again.

Each night brings its inclinations
What it reaps is what we've sown
Endless streets and dancing shadows
Are now my only home
Full of drifting mists and thoughts
And silent screams
Strangers walk by in the half-light
Can they see me too?
Laughter echoes in the dark night
Can they hear me too?
Is it wrong to question why-
Why should I even try?
Wind- blown rain lit by fading streetlights
Casts a spectral glow
Reflected in the eyes of others
Announces it's time to go
To roam whatever may now come
In sepia dreams
Strangers walk by in the half-light
Can they see me too?
Laughter echoes in the dark night
Can they hear me too?
Is it wrong to question why-
Why should I even try?

To live a life within an hour
To feel the coming frost
Where in the bitter scent of a dying flower
Is the price of childhood lost

To feel nostalgia then wear thin
With no rhyme nor reason why
And feel the relentless grasp of Age
As the smile begins to dim

To witness all that ever once had been
Yet can never be again
To doubt that it was ever seen
And hear the falling rain

Older or Younger?

Although I was told I would get older, no-one bothered to tell me how quickly it would happen. It's as though I woke up one morning and there it was, 'Age', stiff joints, bad eyesight, and all the other complaints that some of you may well be familiar with. The loss of mobility, the slowing down, and the fact that a lot of what I enjoyed in previous years is now beyond me should make me angry. Whichever insane deity decided to include physical atrophy as a sign of the years passing ought to be damn well ashamed of them-self. Where once I regarded myself as immortal, it's now been made clear that mortality is going to be a painful process, and a clearly unfair one at that.

That childhood was but fleeting dream
One that now is seldom seen
Where trees became my lofty towers
To look down across those fields of flowers
And every peal of rolling thunder
Battled skies that split asunder
With bolts of flying fire
The children of a greater sire
Such scenes sit deep within my mind
Hidden there, though not maligned
They come, and go, as they do please
Not unlike an autumn breeze
And the question floats before my eyes
Cutting through all binding ties
Where, and why, did those things go?
More to the point, when will I know?

I've never really used mirrors as a guide to my appearance- I was never sure who it was looking back. It seems not only some days that it's becoming harder to recognize the visage reflected, but that those days are beginning to grow in number.

My memories-
They fly with age
As birds escaping
From a cage
Those summers spent
Upon a beach
On Time's tide
They drift from reach
The trees in which
I once did hide
Into stumps
Have been consigned
The sights, and sounds,
I once enjoyed
Have disappeared
By Time destroyed
Where is that child
I once did know-
Was he real,
Where did he go?

What if I'm Not?

A curious thing is the power of imagination, one that might well lead to the question of 'What if I imagined it all? , or even 'What if I, myself am imagined?' René Descartes wrote, when trying to distinguish the difference between *knowledge* and *faith,* 'Dubito, cogito, ergo sum' – or 'I doubt, I think, therefore I am '- to wit – 'We cannot doubt of our existence while we doubt.' But what if he was, in fact, wrong? What if the doubts are not our own but those of the dreamer dreaming us playing out our roles on his stage? Are my memories real, coloured by nostalgia, or mere fantasies? Perhaps, if they are real and everything I write is the truth of my experiences and not someone- or something – else's then are they defining me or am I defining them?

If I say, 'I am', then I must ask 'What am I?' If then this is the case then I must also ask 'Who, and what, are you? ' as much as you should be asking of me?

I am myself
A contradiction
An abrogation, a complication
And most of all
A work of fiction

Watch them as
They come and go
Drifting on
The ebb and flow
They rush as if
They've somewhere to go
Should I care
That they don't know?
How can I be sure that I exist
When the world it turns and twists
And wants to trick me, trick me, trick me
I must be here since I persist
Though the point I may have missed
As they trick me, trick me, trick me
I can't make out
A word they say
It all seems
So far away
Reality
Is so passe
When insanity's
A holiday
How can I be sure that I exist
When the world it turns and twists
And wants to trick me, trick me, trick me
I must be here since I persist
Though the point I may have missed
As they trick me, trick me, trick me
A strange hybrid
Mere portmanteau
Each life played
Adagio
While every day
Passes staccato
With no idea
Of why it's so
How can I be sure that I exist
When the world it turns and twists
And wants to trick me, trick me, trick me
I must be here since I persist
Though the point I may have missed
As they trick me, trick me, trick me

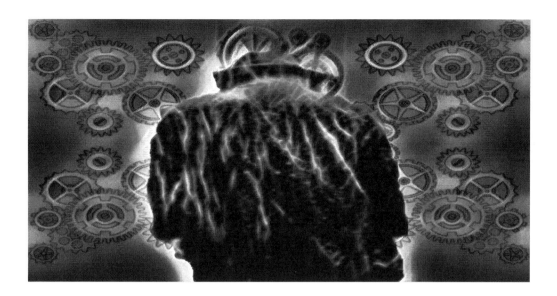

Wandering Dreams and Curious Themes

My childhood, growing up in Mitcham, was spent in books and dreaming of other places for the most part. I didn't really feel part of anything, and even if I had friends if I'm honest I preferred to be sat quietly reading rather than running about outside. Maybe it was a touch of shyness, or a lack of self-confidence, back then but as soon as I was old enough I used to ride the underground to get to museums in London- it seems odd that no matter how busy they were they always seemed to be peaceful, without any noise, and I felt less lost within their confines than I did on the occasions where I found I had to wander the town where I lived.

In my imagination I would travel to places with, of all people, myself – not an alter-ego, mind you, but my actual self and would have conversations about what we had seen or done. Escapism as it may be it helped me to deal with a world that I felt more than remote from for it wasn't a question of not liking the world around me but more one of not understanding it.

If that seems to be a questionable behaviour I can assure you that it wasn't a case of teenage angst, it took me years of conversations –with myself, as insane as it sounds- to actually come to terms with who I was going to be and, once I'd accomplished that, all that remained was to find out why?

So what have you read
That makes you think I'm so wrong?
If you've got questions
Then why've you waited for so long?
This shadow that you see
Has learned to raise its voice
This shadow that you see
Is tired of dreaming
Dreaming
Dreaming
Dreaming
Now

So what have I said
That make you so want to prolong
Hiding your intentions
With such a perfect sense of right and wrong?
This shadow that you see
Has learned to raise its voice
This shadow that you see
Is tired of dreaming
Dreaming
Dreaming
Dreaming
Now

My, how time flies
How much of it is lies?
I'm waiting
Where we begin
Could it be the end?
Still waiting
Still waiting
Still waiting
Still waiting

This shadow that you see
Has learned to raise its voice
This shadow that you see
Is tired of dreaming
Dreaming
Dreaming
Dreaming
Now

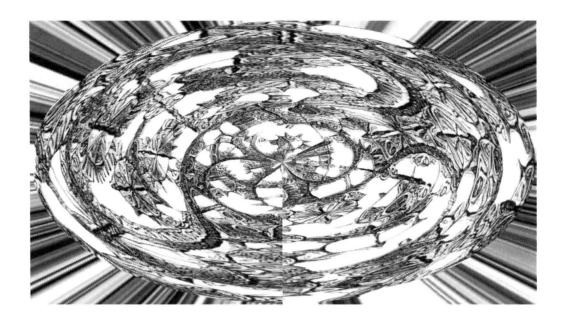

Wednesday's Child

I came into this world, possibly for the first time, on a Wednesday morning in 1966 and, although I can't be sure, I've been told that it was raining with a slight mist. I have some dim memories of the place where I was born, although the prevailing one is of my mother lighting fireworks on the wall of a carpark to entertain us. We moved house a few months after my 3rd birthday, not too far down the road to a place with a garden- oddly it's the garden I remember the most, small as it was, from which we could see the towers at Crystal Palace way off in the distance and they seemed impossibly far away to me at that age. Curiously I ended up, at one point in my life, living not far from them but, sad to say, both they and the park they sit in had lost their mystique by then.

A child of the autumn, born on a Wednesday, yet I seem remarkably free of woes- albeit I do have my cares and worries, mostly those of did I miss the point entirely as to what I should have done?

Wednesday morning promised rain
And as the day took up the strain
I knew that by the time I'd reached the morrow
There'd be nothing left for me to borrow
For age was drawing in

What of the ghosts that are my past?
They come in dreams and always laugh
When I hear my madness call
Asking if I chose to fall
As the clouds come drawing in

Where are my yesterdays?
On stranger winds they drift away
In my Theatre so Absurd
It's almost time to end the play

It seems important nowadays
I wish I knew a better way
Faded faces come and go
Names that I should surely know
Day by day are vanishing

Those childhood mountains I did climb
Were merely molehills now I find
And all those games I used to play
Like the child have passed away
Leaving shadows that grow dim

Where are my yesterdays?
On stranger winds they drift away
In my Theatre so Absurd
It's almost time to end the play

***

Irreverent or irrelevant
A madman, even more
I find myself at peace
Walking on that lonely shore
A stranger path walk I
Where a darker sun does flare
Too late you will come searching
For I am neither here nor there

More or Less

I have a place where, unlike the town of my birth, I don't feel a stranger. It's not where I live now, that's for sure. It's not even in the same county even. There may well be, numbered amongst those of you reading this, some who know me will be aware of where this happens to be. It's not a big place, it's generally quiet, and even if it's decidedly mourning the loss of the former glories that once made it so attractive I still love the place.

For some reason I feel peaceful there. Maybe it's that I can sit and listen to the sea while my world narrows to a singularity – no time but the present, so to speak, and it's the only place where I have ever felt at home. A sanctuary, of sorts, I could quite happily spend the rest of my life there, more or less.

I was told by many
Who I should be
How to think
And what to see
Yet despite all this
I coalesced
Into me, more or less

***

If there was a heaven
It would be close by
Blue seas before us
Beneath wide open skies
What excuse, or reason,
Have we got not to be there?

If I could see heaven
I'd be free of all cares
No need to worry or hurry
Time to stop and just stare
What excuse, or reason,
Have we got not to be there?

If there was a heaven
You could be there too
Free to live out your dreams
To do whatever you choose
What excuse, or reason,
Have we got not to be there?

Ok, it's a bit of a pipe-dream. Nevertheless, it's one that could come true. We all need to dream- I have mine, you have yours, and sometimes it's the simplest ones that come true.

By our thoughts
We shape our worlds
And our heavens
And our hells
Creating all
That we perceive
In order that
We may believe

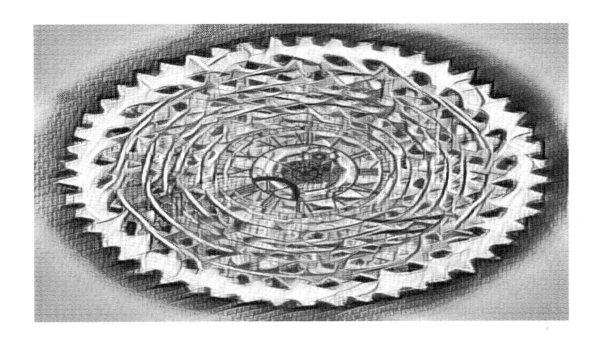

What's the Time?

What's the 'Time'- is it early or late? How much of it do I have left? Days, or years, what's the point of worrying? At the end of it all, one day I'll die but, until then, I'll still be alive for all the days left remaining between now and then left- all that's left to do except make the most of them – to forget about 'time' and just live.

Both past and future
Do so allow
The possibility
That this is 'now'
Although, of course,
It could be 'then'
The problem is
How to know when?

***

Here today, but gone tomorrow-
No time to grieve or walk in sorrow
For somehow
It's always 'now'
Where else could we be?

***

Have I, a child of autumn, already reached the autumn of my life? How far away is winter, and does it really have to come?

Fading flowers
Gentle breeze
What waits behind
This strange new dream?
Where will you be
Once I have gone
Far beyond
My autumn's song?

***

I've watched my Self
As Time walks by
Understanding neither
How or why
When I ask my Self,
'How goes the day?'
That no reply
Does come my way

***

Upon the ship
That sails my mind
Not a soul there
Will you find
For the crew
Found a new direction
And drowned in seas
Of introspection

Reculver

Reculver is a place from my early childhood, on the Kent coast not far from Margate. Surprisingly those memories of it are still clear – of pebble beaches, thick seaweed, assorted pieces of cuttlefish and other detritus washed up on the shore, and of a tiny caravan back in the days when gas lamps were quite normal to find in such a thing.

A week, that's how long we went for, just a week but it felt so very much longer and we did what we did to keep ourselves amused. I'm going back there, for a day, this year- to take a last look at the place, for it's doubtful I'll ever go back again, in the hope that maybe I'll hear an echo or two from those years gone by.

If anything, it's to convince myself they actually happened because I'm starting to have my doubts.

Once I scratched my name
Upon some sea tossed stone
But when I went to find it
It was lost beneath the foam

***

A tiny piece of Heaven
Perched atop a cliff
Seagulls skimming waves
Blown by breeze so stiff
Rocks, pebbles, washed up junk
Nothing was ignored
To our minds it was precious
And had to be explored
That place had the power
To hold us all day long
Yet we left it all behind
And only now we see the wrong
For in those shades of childhood
We never know the cost
Or that the passing years
Would leave our Paradise lost

***

Too late it seems that now I find
Those memories but one step behind
That dog my steps this very day
Are the words I could not say

***

My future Self
It does ask why
It seems the past
Has passed me by?

***

There is a room in which I find
All the seashells of my mind
Where thoughts can spiral, even flare
And some so briefly do play there
Others though, with footfall stronger
Walk around and stay much longer

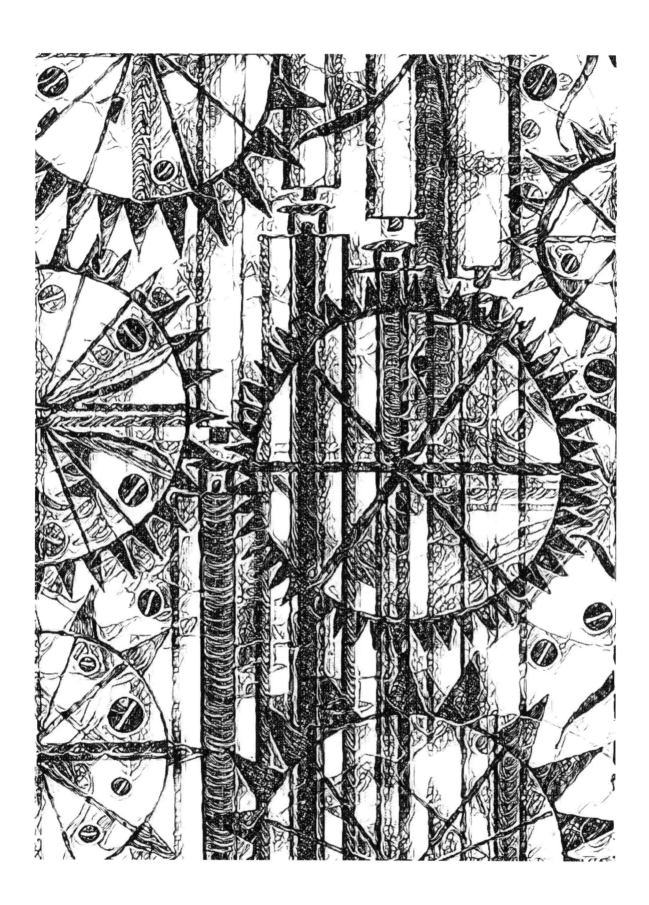

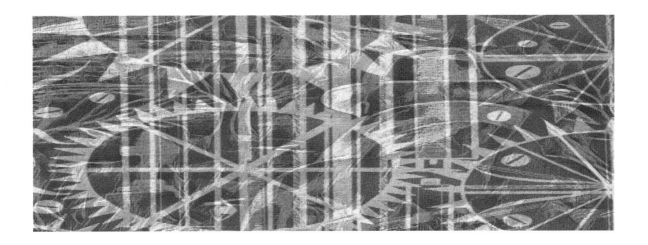

Into the Trees

A great deal of my childhood was spent in trees, mostly perched on some branch or other reading whatever book I had managed to lay my hands on. How I managed to climb some of them I can only guess- it's a feat far beyond my capabilities nowadays. Some of them still stand whilst some, rather sadly, do not.

I often wondered back then, and still do even now, is if trees are conscious then what thoughts do they have? Considering their lifespan would their minds be slow and ponderous, as fast as ours, or even faster? What would the dreams of trees be like, or their nightmares? Mostly though, if they are aware of us, in the same way as we are of them, would those trees I remember so well remember me?

Tree I climbed
Its branches high
For as a child
My world was wide
And all I saw
Was strange and new
How I loved
That wind-blown view
From my tower
In the sky
Where I sat
With open eye

***

Of what was once my favourite tree
There is little left to see
Killed it was by poisoned air
And no-one even seems to care

****

Where do memories go
As we fade with age?
Is it merely passing time
Or do we place them in a cage?
Where do memories go
Once they pass beyond the gate?
Can we recover them
Or is it simply far too late?
Where do memories go
To where are they consigned?
Or are they merely wandering
In the forests of my mind?

***

Old Yew tree
Your roots do go
Down to where
Dark waters flow
What there then
Do you hope to see
Now all the children have left
Yes, even me

***

Willow tree, my sanctuary
How many years together did we see?
Dreaming dreams within your fronds
But that child is now long gone
And though the river still flows nothing is the same
Except the pain
Why is your voice
Now silent?

In dreams you come and go
But from where I cannot know
Time appeared and broke our bonds
Now I no longer hear your songs
And though the river still flows nothing is the same
Except the pain
Why is your voice
Now silent?

Memories are all that now remain
Part of my life's long broken chain
Where I came from no longer exists
Though the rumour still persists
And though the river still flows nothing is the same
Except the pain
Why is your voice
Now silent?

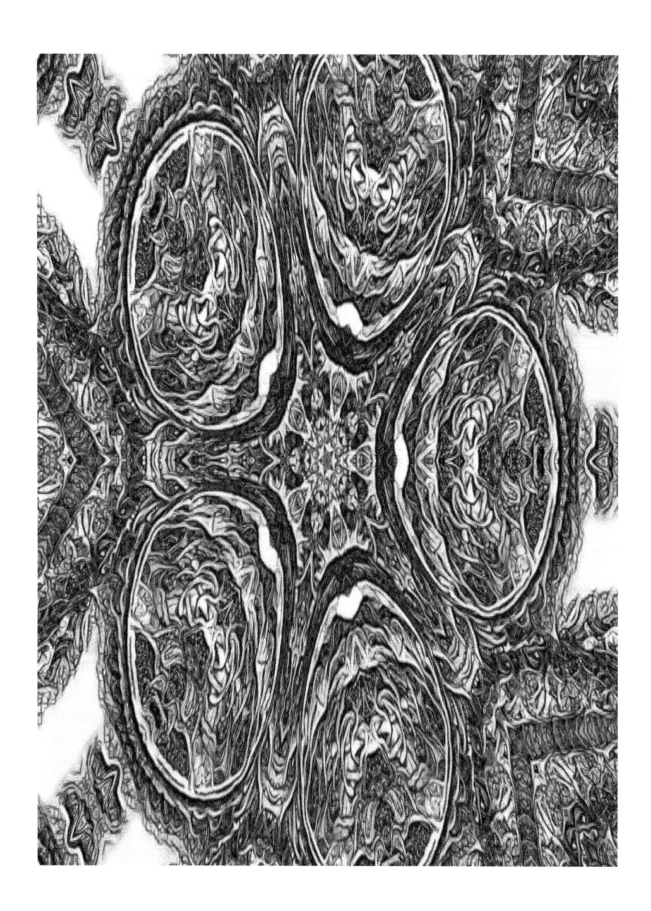

Chains

Dickens' had Jacob Marley describing the chains that weighed him down as being forged by the actions committed during his life- as a child I loved the story , especially the Alastair Sim's film version and for a long time I wondered exactly what the meaning of the chains was.

Young as I was the message of goodwill to all men all year round was fairly clear, yet I began to wonder if we carried 'chains' in life as well – cares, worries, regrets, even childhood hopes and dreams. Could such things sustain us as adults by means of appearing as memories, or would they hold as back? Fast approaching my fifty-second year on this earth I should have some idea of the answer yet, odd as it may seem, I don't.

One day there may come to me
The reason why that I should be
For then with foresight
I can leave behind
The chains of the past
That bind my mind
And perhaps
Be free

***

What follows then
So close behind?
'Tis the chains of my past
There I do find
That whisper quietly
In my mind

***

Random thought
You shall so fade
Passing quietly
On your way
Neither here
Nor even there
Drifting through
My night, my day
Wordlessly
Without a thought
Chained by the past
We both are caught

***

Time is an infection
Contracted by those who deserve it least
Weighed down by the chains of introspection
We learn the nature of the beast
Always hungering for more
Yet no longer welcome at the feast

***

Link by link
We forge our chain
Yet even when broken
It stays the same

***

It's the final joke
One we should have detected
Time's a disease
And we're all infected!

***

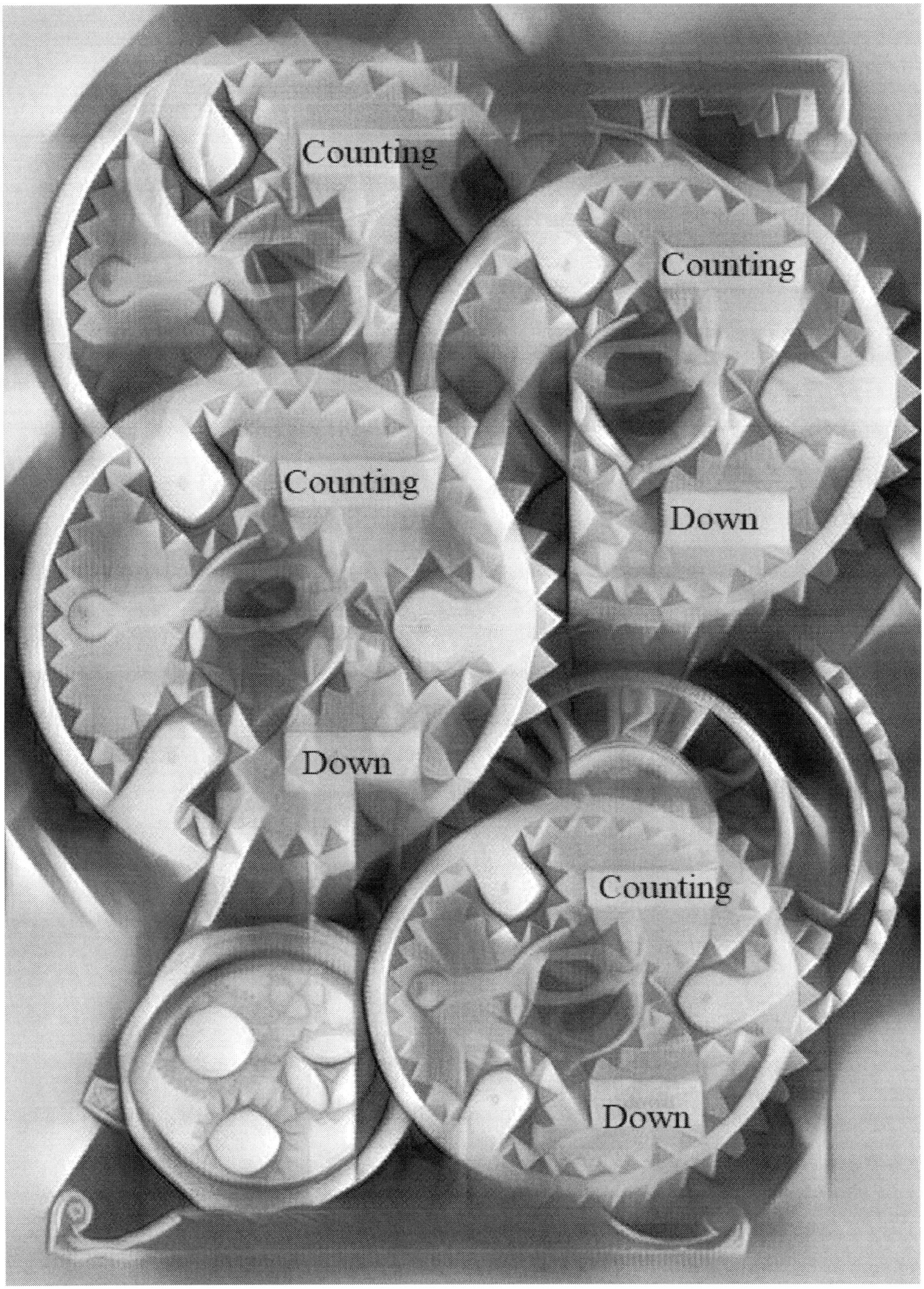
Counting
Counting
Counting
Down
Down
Counting
Down

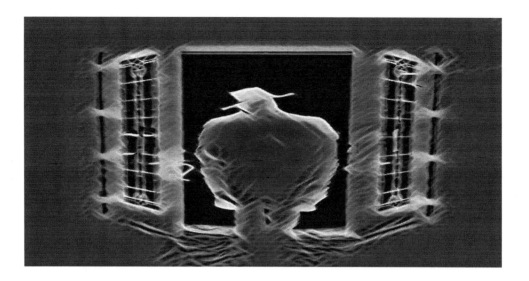

Counting the Days

I've already lived through six decades, something I find incredible, who would have thought it? All sorts of things have changed- some good, some bad, some that just seem to have been better left the way they are. Progress, if it can be called that, is inevitable yet to my mind at least it appears that there are people who seem to look for a way to destroy anything that's good and replace with what may be politely described as ' a policy of modernisation' – charmless, grey, sprawling, nightmares that have no place in our worlds.

Look at your childhood and try to remember the places you knew- the parks, the seaside resorts, even the streets and roads you walked down, where are they now? Those places don't exist anymore- they've been altered, some subtly, some beyond understanding, so why not ask your -self why?

One day, hopefully, I'll find a place that still is the world my childhood took part in- one that hasn't been destroyed by developers and architects that have no sympathy or understanding of the area they want to become as soulless as they are. It's just a matter of time, it has to be out there somewhere, and I'm counting the days till I find it.

How can you be so sure
That you were ever there
When what you see now
Causes such despair?

***

I watched my childhood
On a beach
Though it was near
It was out of reach
I tried to take it
By the hand
As it danced
Across the sand
Drifting on the winds and tide
As beneath horizon
The sun did slide
Yet by the light
Of rising moon
Came a thought
And all too soon
I realized that
My shadow had changed
And never more
Could be the same
Thus my world
Revealed its flaw
With icy seeds
Placed in my core
The wreckage then
Of what once was me
Passed with the tides
That moves Time's sea
Far beyond
My memory's sight
And left me there
Alone in the night

***

Beyond the Sea
Of memories
There sat you
Alone with me
By sadness bound
And melancholic
For the past it was
Almost hypnotic
What need was there
To so append
The urge to countdown
To the end
When together we sang
Our Autumn's song
Knowing that soon
We'd both
Be gone

***

The thought that came
Of late to me
A memory of
All I have seen
Where is that place
That for now I long?
I did not stay
And forgot its song

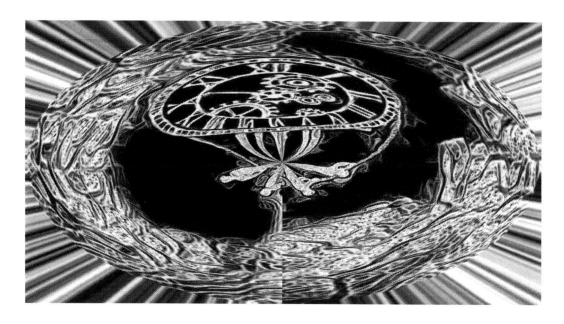

Because!

One day, unless of course I'm wrong, I shall die and, in time, be forgotten. It will be as if I never existed, few will notice my passing and fewer still be concerned. We all wish to leave some trace of who we were, what we did, behind and in my case it's my books that I hope will be a monument of sorts. The thought than in the years to come a stranger may come across my work, read it, understand it , and enjoy it, is a comforting thought even.

It's a curious thing for once, a few years back, I was asked at a book launch, 'Why do you write? Are you trying to become famous?' The only reply I could honestly give was,' No, it's because'.

Once I saw a sparrow fall
From its perch in tree so tall
To others it remained unseen
A life that may have never been
And I questioned why this was?
But there was no answer
Except
Because

***

In time the Earth
Will observe my fall
And with great care
Cover it all

***

Book you lead to other worlds
And I am grateful so
For this one is wearing thin
And soon from it I must go

***

'Tis a strange, peculiar, sadness
That afflicts my soul
A disease that has no cure
Yet it makes me whole
Appearing without warning
Forming mists before my eyes
Watching each day passing
And seeing how time flies

***

Take me then
Wherever you will
Whether 'tis under
Or over the hill
Take me then
So that I may dream
As I am leaving
For that place unseen

***

Age now so freely mocks me
With a certain flair
And as my years are growing
My memories despair
As they ask of us the questions
'Were we ever really there?'

Changes

I have changed over the years, and not just in size or shape- my personality has too. Where once I felt I had to move at speed I can now move at a more leisurely pace and not worry about how others may view my actions. It may just be the fact that I've got older, but the urge to rush anything has long since passed and I'm far happier for it.

It's almost like being a kid again- I can stop and stare at anything that takes my eye and enjoy the sense of wonder or appreciation that comes with it. Have I mellowed out, absolutely- even if I'm not that mad about Saffron. Then again it could all be down to the meds.

Such changes are
I find inclined
To sneak up slowly
From behind
But to them I'll
Still raise a glass
And tell the world
To kiss my arse

***

If, with time, you see I've changed
Can you know of why
When from my youth I am estranged
And see a different sky?
No longer do I so aspire
To my childhood dreams
For to what I did so once desire
Proved to be so different from my needs

***

For Fate sits and so devises
So many, sometimes strange, surprises
To prove that when Life's tale unfolds
It's never quite as you've been told

***

Where once I played on swings,
Roundabouts and slides
Nowadays it's impossible-
I've gotten far too wide
And all those playground thrills
Are sadly out of reach
For the years have made me like a whale
Stuck upon a beach

***

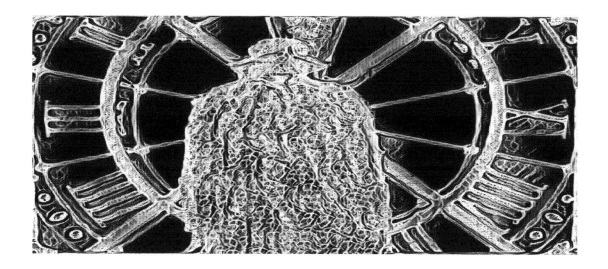

It's Later than We Think

There was a thought to title this chapter 'Five Minutes to Midnight', but I settled on what you see above. This close to the end of the book, and at this time of night when the day has run its course I'm left wondering if I'll ever come across anyone from my past because of my books and what would they make of them? More to the point what would they make of me now? Would I be surprised by how they had changed, if they had at all, or vice versa? Where did they all go to? How did we lose touch?

What about you then? Are there people you've lost touch with – friends, family, whoever? Why not spare a few seconds to think about them- then perhaps see if you can find them online, or someone who might know of them. It's worth giving it a go, if only to say hello. Do it while you have time to try, because it's later than we thought.

Tell me where you went to
And have the years been kind?
What are your hopes and worries?
Whatever's on your mind
We could sit and talk
About what we used to do
The things that made us laugh
Of everything that's new

***

Seconds, minutes, hours
Away from us they flow
Turning into years
What right have they to go?
Days, and weeks, and months
Become nothing but a blur
As half remembered memories
Come dimly to the fore
If only we knew then
What we all know now
Perhaps things might be different
Would we the future disallow?
But what has passed has passed
To it we are a dying link
There's less of us each day
And it's later than we think

***

The moving hands
Upon that clock
Will not slow
Until they stop
They have their purpose
And they care not
That it unravels
Fate's dark knot

***

Behind us all there is a path
That can only once be walked
It hides within our memories
And about it we've often talked

The End of the Road

This is it- the final day. For this is now the end of the road and I've done all I can. Looked back, checked over everything, tripped over here and there but still managed to rise and carry on, and believe me it's a strange feeling to know there's nothing left to do. Except see what comes next- which, of course, is all any of us can do and hope what we've left behind makes some sense to those who will come after us.

As for the past, are we remembering what happened, what we would have liked to have happened, or even what we can only hope didn't occur other than in a nightmare? Maybe that's what we find out when we finally reach the end of the road.

The road of which my childhood formed such a tiny part
Is rarely travelled nowadays though I do not lack the heart
For the myth of age and time
Have robbed me of the strengths that I once had
Yet if I could return there then surely I'd be glad

***

The wreckage of my childhood
Away from me flows
But I could never warn myself
For I could not have known
And the past always reminds me
That there will be
No tomorrow
For I can see
The end of the road

The wreckage of my thoughts
Have nowhere left to go
Whatever you may think
I didn't reap quite as I sowed
Yet the days seem to keep on moving
As the years
Keep on growing
And I can see
The end of the road

***

Though we have reached the end my friend
Still there's so much left to say
But to do so we must hope
We can survive another day

***

DW STORER

PSYCHIC . AUTHOR . CHAINSMOKER

The official site for author DW Storer.

Read. Think. Discuss.

dwstorer-author.uk

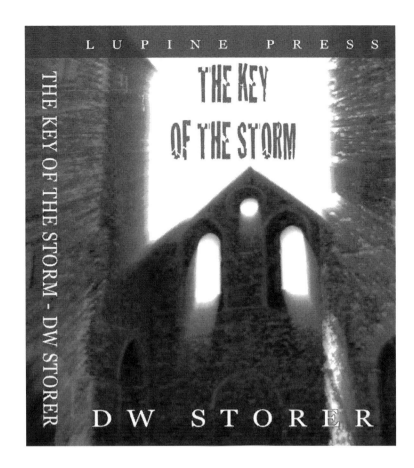

Available as E-Reader and paperback on Amazon
The Key of the Storm raises the curtains on the darkly provocative trilogy, Through the Mirror Darkly.

Comforted by a powerful mystic as he observes the grisly conclusion to his death, DW Storer's autobiographical antihero is taken on a journey of classical proportions, as he absorbs, celebrates, and ultimately confronts lessons learned during the dawning of his afterlife.

Set in a timeless astral plane that is home to an exotic array of gods, kings, queens, ferocious beasts, historical figures and tortured souls, Storer includes factual accounts of his spiritual development and encounters with entities, both benign and malevolent, to reinforce his central tenet that even the most finely tuned will is susceptible to otherworldly temptation.

The second book in the Through The Mirror Darkly Series

Available as E-Reader and paperback on Amazon

Poems Without A Home is not a conventional work - it comes from a soul roaming free from the body that is a witness to the darkness that exists beyond the consciousness and observes 'other' realities where unheard voices demand their pain to be known

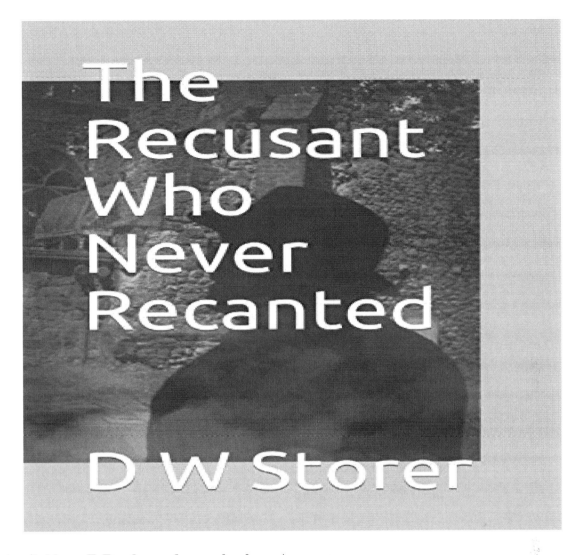

Available as E-Reader and paperback on Amazon

This is the 3rd book in the Through the Mirror Darkly quadrilogy - and continues the story began in The Key of The Storm -formed of two parts -

part 2 ,The Recusant Who Never Recanted sees the Storm tempt the Celt with the opportunity to pass judgement on those perceived to be evil - yet to do so would save few in the attempt to create a more just world.

D W Storer's unique style of antique prose and dark poetry takes the reader back into uncharted territory where a subtle venom questions and tests all faiths, beliefs, and moralities even at the very end

For children –

Available as E-Reader and paperback on Amazon

With only seven sleeps 'till Christmas Blue Ted is too excited to sleep - find out how Bedtime Bear helps him - easy to follow poetry with simple rhymes - sure to delight your child as you read along with them

Printed in Great Britain
by Amazon